Penelope's Purple Passions

The Emergence of The Butterfly

PENELOPE CHAISSON

EVOKE180 PUBLISHING | LAUDERHILL, FL

Copyright © 2021 by **Penelope Chaisson**

All rights reserved. No part of this publication may be reproduced, distributed or transmitted in any form or by any means, without prior written permission.

Penelope Chaisson/Evoke180 Publishing
Lauderhill, FL
www.evoke180.com

Publisher's Note: This is a work of fiction. Names, characters, places, and incidents are a product of the author's imagination. Locales and public names are sometimes used for atmospheric purposes. Any resemblance to actual people, living or dead, or to businesses, companies, events, institutions, or locales is completely coincidental.

Penelope's Purple Passions/ Penelope Chaisson.
ISBN 978-1-7377826-0-5

Acknowledgments

I would like to begin by acknowledging my mother, Warrine Chaisson, who took me to the library to get my first library card and ignited my love for reading and expressing myself on the pages of paper as a young girl. I would also like to thank a friend of mine, who is a poet, for reminding me of how much I love poetry. A special thanks also to all of my close friends and gym buddies who have supported me on this journey.

Dedication

To my beautiful daughter Amber, whose sweet spirit and smile always fills me with so much joy.

Many thanks to my family for their support .

I would like to thank all my friends who read my countless poems and believed in me and encouraged me.

Lastly, thanks to my publisher and his wife for their unwavering support during this time that my book was being birthed.

Contents

Acknowledgments v
Dedication vii

The Egg's Innocence
Eyes Of Fire 2
Watching 4
What's Behind It All? 5
The Daze 7
Adrift 9
Shadow Catcher 10
You Are What I See When I Look at the Sky's Blue 11
Live 12
Silence 14
Dreamcatcher 16
First Date 18
The Game 22

The Larvae's Sincerity
Mind Teaser 26
Burning Love 27
Wet Dream 28
Visions 29
Love's Kiss 31
What's Real? 33
Confused 35
Home 36
Losing 37
Time 39
Escape 41
Lonely 42

No Explanations 43
Now 45

The Pupa's Paradigm Shift
You Don't Know Me. 48
Judged 50
A Fool 52
The Joke's on Me 53
Blind 55
Love 57
Truth 59
The Zone. 60
Thinking. 62
The Airport. 64
Write Back When You Get My Letter 66
Lay With It 69
No Delete Button. 70
Your Loss 71
Morning Comes. 73
Ghosts. 74

The Adult's Climax
Sorry 76
Let Go 78
Rainbows 79
Destiny 81
Madness, Maybe. 83
Unfamiliar Face 85
Seven Years 88
Wednesday. 90
New Leaf. 92
Impression. 94
Thankful. 96
Butterfly Wings 97

About Penelope Chaisson. 99

Penelope's Purple Passions is a story of the butterfly who innocently falls in love only to find out that love can be complicated, and that it changes and evolves just as she does. She is about to embark upon a life-changing journey—one of self-discovery, transformation, and evolution. Once the butterfly accepts that everything is about growth and evolution, she views her journey differently. It's as though someone has given her a new lens to see through, and now her vision is clear for her expectations of life, love, and self-worth. Then, there's the ultimate realization that without the hardships and growing pains, she would not have been able to transform into the beautiful butterfly that she sees when she looks into the mirror.

The Egg's Innocence

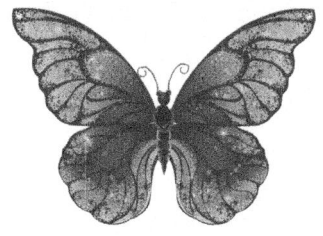

Eyes Of Fire

Who is it?
I see beyond those blazing spellcasters.

Captivating, intoxicating . . .
they definitely have me mesmerized.
But who is it really behind those eyes?
You drew me in,
and all the breath left my body,
like a corpse.
You left me with nothing
but nakedness.

Your eyes possess the power
to do whatever they will with me.
They speak to me.
They hold me.
They caress me.

There's something about those eyes!
I've tried to break away,
but when they summon me
I'm like a zombie,
I must submit.

They make the magnificently pieced together
symphonies of Beethoven seem so minuscule.

I've never in my life
seen such eyes as these.
You have my attention now.
You have full authority over me.

I can no longer fight you off.
Your supreme dominance
leaves your subjects lifeless.

And as for me,
I want to remain hypnotized

by your spell.

I enjoy this prison you've laid before me.
I'm like an empty creation
in the sculptor's hands
when it comes to you.

Your eyes pierce through me.
They've influenced the person I've come to be.

Watching

And there they were, watching. They're always watching my full lips, the power of my hips, the round curves that hug my waist, the firmness of my butt, and the way it stacks up against my black workout jacket. I can imagine the thoughts dancing in their heads as they say to themselves, "This lady's one hell of a statuesque package."

What's Behind It All?

What's behind their eyes?
    Don't be fooled by the innocent glare.
Deep beneath the surface are many lies,
a pool of pain, love, wonder, and mystery in a stare.

But how can anyone see or love the real you
when all you do is hide behind closed doors?

Behind each door
    lies a film of thick smoke no one can see through.
Broken pieces spread across
    nicely polished wooden floors.

A plethora of information
waiting there just for me to take hold.
If I could reach the pinnacle of this human existence,
I could free myself from our two connected souls.

But my eyes have caught a glimpse of the future.
My tongue has tasted the beauty that lies before.

My eyes close at night and dream
of being with you, and I desire nothing more.

How long will you continue to stare at me,
and strip me bare with your beautiful brown eyes?

Will you ever conjure up the nerve to approach me
and say something,
or will you just sit back and let the years roll by?

The Daze

Right now, I'm getting so frustrated,
very aggravated.

Sometimes, I feel like I'm going out of my mind.
Is this all your magnificent design?

I feel as though I'm being tortured alive,
navigating this maze you forced me to suffer through.
My love goes beyond skin deep
when it comes to being with you.

I often find myself wandering around
speaking to myself like a crazy person,
in a sort of daze
not being able to pick apart the game that's being played.

I'm pretty sure you know exactly
what you're doing to me.
This is why you have me running around
like a wild coyote chasing its tail
pursuing you blindly.

There's something about when your eyes meet mine
that leaves me in a trancelike state.

Then I think,
I'm not supposed to escape;
I'm the bait.

Adrift

I dream of you
when I look out my bedroom window at night
into the powder blue sky.
My mind wanders off,
and it somehow always drifts
right back to you.

I don't know why,
but your face, your voice, your smile,
the way you walk,
it's always you.

Shadow Catcher

Have you ever fallen in love with a shadow?
I know it sounds weird, even unbelievable.
I fell in love with the illusion
of being with your shadow.
I started obsessing and desiring to know,
when it gets exhausted, where does it go?
Did it disappear to warm bubble baths at night?
Soothing scents of lavender and such delights?
Did it wait for someone to come home
and caress it softly at night?
A shadow catcher like myself
often ponders thoughts like those.
I look for your shadow in everything that I do
and in every place that I go.

You Are What I See When I Look at the Sky's Blue

You don't even realize the power
I've surrendered to you with ease.
Like a great big ocean, you engulf me,
and I'm the waves you toss back and forth,
however you please.

Your very presence overwhelms me.
It's like trying to measure
the breadth and width of the sea.

During my resting hours,
when I'm supposed to be asleep with my eyes closed,
I tuck you away, close to my heart, safely,
so your spirit always has a place to go.
Someone once said to me, "If you make a wish,
and you want it bad enough, it will come true."
But I prefer to stay in my dreams forever,
adrift like a shipwrecked sailor;
that way, I can always be with you.

Live

You make me want to live again.
There's no time or space, just the awe of you, and
I'm living.

Your smile envelops my body like a blanket, so softly.

I awake to breakfast in bed with you
and a cup of roasted Colombian coffee.

Only you have that way
of tearing down
all my papier-mâché walls.

Over the years,
I had built a protective fortress around me,
but you're able to expose my emotions.

I don't want to fall off the edge
into love's arms.
I don't want to be led on by you
and end up harmed.

Love is a sacred place,
from which many souls do not return whole.

The Egg's Innocence

I don't want to be vulnerable to you,
lose all sense of control.

I'm not even sure how all of this transpired.
I never saw any of it coming.
I was just going about my life in a normal way,
until you passed me that day,
and now, I'm a lovestruck woman.

Silence

Some say silence is golden.
To that cliché, I can attest,
for I've kept silent
for about three years at best.

In silence,
much knowledge can be attained.
Many things can be appreciated,
like the pouring down
of a chilly April's rain.

I can hear the bird's singing
in the early morning hours
while the dew is still wet on the grass.
If you don't know how to embrace silence,
these things come and then they pass.

In my silence,
I've seen snowflakes dropping on the concrete
and watched them dissolve into water
when they hit the rubble on the ground.

All of this magic happens
when there's an absence of sound,
no distractions or people conversing all around.

The laughter of children playing inside the schoolhouse
on a cold and dreary day.

They sing lyrics like, "Rain, rain, go away,
come again another day, little Sally wants to play,
rain, rain, go away."

In my silence,
I was also able to see you,
the love of my life, my summer's day,
my someone in the winter to have and to hold.

I'm hoping when you find out
how much I care for you,
the warmth of my heart will meet your heart,
welcomed and unopposed.

Dreamcatcher

My dreams are quite different than most.

They take flight after dark
and are filled with mysteries and adventures,
even tales of ghosts.

I love to live there in my fairy tales;
that's my designated sacred time alone.

It's there that I can create whatever I want, a secret world of my own.

It's in my dreams that my imagination is set free,
so it can create and flow.

In my imagination, I've built a safe castle where all captive lovers can go.

I waited for my lover one night,
at the lighthouse called Lady Divine

I sent a distress signal out toward the shore,
so I would be easy to find.

The Egg's Innocence

It was like a game of hide-and-seek,
and when I looked up, my lover stood right behind me.

It kind of blew my mind
the way it happened expeditiously.

How did you arrive so quickly?
I sent the sirens out just now.

My lover said,
"Remember, I'm a part of your imagination.
In your dreams, you get to determine the when
and the how."

First Date

It was going to be our first night
spending time alone together.
I guess you could call it a kind of "date,"
or whatever.

I was all worked up the whole day
because I couldn't wait.
Some alone time with you
was something I had longed for
and anticipated.

We decided we would ride together
and grab a few drinks at a bar.
We caught a cab there together
because it was close to my job,
not really that far.

We sat there talking,
getting to know each other, intimately.
My hands were sweating,
and my heart was racing.

The thought of being alone with you
intimidated me.

The Egg's Innocence

Sitting there, playing with my fingernails,
I tried to play it cool.
In my head, I kept telling myself to relax,
don't blow it
by acting like a fool.

I took a few deep breaths,
inhale, exhale.
I practiced my breathing
like I was doing hot yoga.
My palms were sweaty as hell.

I looked at my watch for a second;
it seemed like the time was moving so fast.
I didn't want to go home anytime soon.

I was with you,
and I wanted the night to last.

I can be very taciturn at times,
but I didn't want you to get the impression
that I couldn't carry on a conversation.

So I sat there, tongue-tied,
thinking about what I should say to you.

It had been years
since I seriously dated someone, and I was so rusty with

this whole dating scene. But I got the feeling
you were just as nervous as me.

Every time we looked at each other,
we smiled with a nervous grin.
We were so into each other,
and it was written all over our faces.

I told you that night
that I didn't frequent bars or any such places
We just continued to stare at each other,
looking like we were in love.

I just let the conversation flow
and the chips fall where they needed to fall.
My chair was pulled close to yours,
and your back faced the wall.

We sat at the bar, savoring our drinks timidly.
I asked you what you were having to drink,
and then you reached over and gave yours to me.

I'm not sure if you were testing me,
to see if I was too scared to take a sip from your glass.

But I did,
and it was good.

And you followed my lips
as they glided around the rim of your glass.
I guess I passed.

I didn't know what to think.
At last, I felt like we were really bonding
on that deeper level now.
Then I felt your thigh brush up against mine,
and I felt an electrical current, and I was like, "Wow."

I thought,
*What in the world would have happened
if we had connected on that night?* You know,
 intimately, passionately,
as one would say, on that mind-blowing level.

In that moment,
our bodies had this amazing language
that we both could certainly feel.
And I wanted to lose control to you,
hand over the keys of my self-will.

I was there,
in what felt like a never-ending
dreamlike state.
That was the night we met up at the bar
at a quarter to eight.

The Game

I remember the day exactly,
when I felt like, *Hey,*
is there something going on between us here?

I was a little tickled and embarrassed at first,
but then my heart started to pound with fear.

At first, I thought it was all in my head,
your subtle, sophisticated flirting,
and then I became a little afraid.

Whenever you would pass by,
I would try to hide.

I didn't want my facial expressions
to give me away.

I was so filled with pride.

It was so new and exciting,
all at the same time too.

And I kind of enjoyed
playing this game with you.

But it's not much fun
when you're the hunted one,
and the hunter is done.

Your gazes,
how you touched the small of my back,
all of these close encounters,
left my nerves exposed.

I'm not sure
what drove you so hard and fast
and made you pull away just the same.
I'm not sure if you were ever really in it
or if it was all just a game.

The Larvae's Sincerity

Because nobody wanted me to have you, it made me want you even more.

Mind Teaser

Thoughts pacing up and down in my mind,
not keeping up with time
That's what happens when my mind drifts off to you.

Today, I saw someone standing up on the subway.
He turned around and smiled my way.
He had the same sexy silhouette as you.

His hair was jet black and fine,
just like yours, and suddenly I was frozen in time.
Eventually, all roads lead back to you.

Why did I pause?
We both know the cause.
It's because my mind and body
still cry out for you.

Burning Love

You know exactly what to do.
You entice a person,
drawing them closer and closer to you.
It's just that this foolish heart has its own mind.

I mean,
it's not like I don't know I'm wasting my time.

My silly heart won't stop pursuing you.
It rules my entire being.
I have no power over it.
I'm like a piece on the chessboard.
All of my moves are controlled,
and there's no fleeing.

Don't you know, if I could,
I would just turn around and run away?
You started this fire years ago
and kept it slowly burning.
And now my broken heart yearns to stay.

Wet Dream

Wet dream. It's about the time before the time that never really happens. Sweat dripping down my back, the anticipation, this has got to be a fatal attraction. Warm water running in the bathroom shower. Steam filled the glass with a fog-like appearance for about an hour. Hands stroking my honey-brown skin, moving up and down my spine. I told you I don't like being choked for the last time. So much power in those hands. It's hard to understand. You back me against the shower. The strong force from your body, I'm loving all that power. I especially love the feeling of your tongue as you kiss my mouth fervently.

I've reached the mountain's peak; All of my defenses are down; I've gotten weak. Then, I wake up from this wet dream, hoping to see you. Wait, is this dream over? Are we through? You are not here. And I fear you may be off somewhere, loving someone else. And deep inside, I wish it was me. But I can't help it; my wet dream melts like a soggy ice cream cone. I realize it was only a dream, and I'm actually here all alone.

Visions

Visions of your soft wet lips
pressed tightly against my hips,
at last.
I'm really living in the moment now.
I'm not thinking about anything from my past.

Slow, soft music on an old vinyl record player
sounded from an open window.
There we'd lie together outside on a hot summer's day,
kissing slowly,
our warm-blooded bodies pressed tightly against each
other on a bed of rose petals in the grass.
You loved to look at nature,
And I loved lying in your arms watching the time pass.

I just never could get into the bugs,
but I understood they had a purpose on the planet too.
That's who you were, that light in this world,
with eyes so bright.
That's what made me fall in love with you.
With your beautiful smile,
you reminded me of those carefree days
when I was my happiest as a child.

You brought out the silly in me.
I would just smile for no reason.
You were my summer, fall, autumn, winter,
all of my seasons.

Why you disappeared and left me?
I guess I'll never know.
And now, it's a chilly winter's night in Colorado.

And I'm standing here looking out my window,
daydreaming, watching the snow.

I'm still hoping,
waiting for your next arrival.

But until that day,
I guess I'll have to wait around and settle.

Love's Kiss

This is the thing about true love's kiss.
Nobody knows when it will strike, who it will land on, or
who it will miss.

You're never given a choice.
You come into complete submission
when you encounter this force.

You cannot see.
You're left without a voice, only the ability to feel.

It leads you out onto a dark, lonely, abandoned road,
driving a car without a steering wheel.

You're like a ship left out at sea,
and you wonder if there's anybody out there
who feels this same way too.

Perhaps they will come and rescue you?
There's never a warning sign that says,
"Look out! There's danger behind you"
or "don't get in too deep."

I'm being tossed about to and fro,
like a ship with a broken sail in the night hours,
not getting any sleep.
Let me come up for air at least.
Let me catch my breath please.

Is there anyone out there who can hear me?

I fooled around this time
and accepted an innocent kiss,
and now love's kiss is haunting me.

What's Real?

I thought I had loved many until I met you.
Then I realized that none of my other loves could have
been true.
None of the others had felt like you.
My love never wavered; it was steady through
and through.
And although I yearn to feel that way again,
something within always makes me feel as though my
loving you was a sin.
And then.
There is the new day that comes after every other day.
Then I gain the strength and courage and begin to feel
like it's okay.
I mean, to have loved another soul this way.
I can't begin to explain the intense gravity of how I felt.
It was like watching a giant white marshmallow
on a wooden stick over the fireplace melt.
It was hot, and soft, and it left me satisfied and content.
And I bit into it; I had a taste.
It felt good sliding into my mouth,
smooth on my tongue,
so sweet and I knew what it meant.
I savored every bit, and then it was gone.
But I kept wanting more and more.

The tension built up inside me, the deep anticipation of
what else might be in store.
Beyond what I could touch, taste, or feel.
You were lying here with me,
and it was not a fairy tale, you were real.

Confused

They told me they would always love me.
At least that's what I thought the message they
sent meant.
Was I to be blamed because I found them fascinating
and innocent?
I can't help it; there was so much mystery their
presence brought.
I felt we had a deep soul connection, at least that's what
I thought.
Sometimes feelings and emotions without words can be
such a tricky thing.
I didn't want to be a one-night stand; I wanted to be
their everything.

Home

You always felt like home to me. From the first time I looked into your brown eyes, and you blushed bright red with a coy, innocent, childlike smile, you always felt like home to me. That's why I hurried to place myself directly in your path. Since I knew you always passed by the long corridor in the mornings, you always felt like home to me. That's why I would stay up until the late hours of the night styling my hair and getting my clothing just right. In the anticipation that I would run into you the next day, you always felt like home to me. That's why I would wait until you walked past me in the mornings just to say hi and see your face up close.

You always felt like home to me. That is why I would write by candlelight during the late hours of the night with only the thought of you in sight. You always felt like home to me. That is why I would lay myself down to sleep and make a wish that if I could only keep one thing, it was always you. Now, when I wait and anticipate the day you will return with your heart open to me, it will be because you've always been home to me, and you always will be.

Losing

I feel like I'm losing you
with every breath that leaves my weakened body.
I don't want to let you go.
This is why I'm holding on so tightly.

I'm not finished with what we never started
or had a chance to begin.
You darted right out of my life
as quickly as you came in.

And I centered photos of you perfectly,
    deeply embedded in my mind.
I don't think I'll ever forget your name.
I remember one night, I played a game.

I placed all the facts of what I wanted in a mate,
things only a real lover could appreciate.
I stayed up until midnight, kind of late.

So instead of staying up, pacing the house,
I decided to find out what this mystery was about.
    I took an online quiz
    called Guess Who It Is?
    I took a chance,

and what happened next was crazy.
It revealed that my crush's name started with
the letter G.
It freaked me out, stunned because of what it said.

All along, I had known it was you, in my head.
   I couldn't approach you of course.
I was never that bold
   because,
as the universe had already foretold,
one day you and I would surely meet.

We were on a collision course with destiny.
Sure enough, I got a text from you,
and I didn't believe it was real.

How could you possibly know how I feel?
I guess the stars and the moon
and the whole earth really do conspire
to fulfill our heart's true desires.
I know because it brought me you,
and for that I'll forever be grateful.

Time

If I could but just for a minute in my mind,
stop the ticktock of the clock, rewind.
The only two factors in this math equation would be
you and me.
The gentle breeze from the sea water on the beach
blew us together one day.
You were walking barefoot on the sand,
and you looked up and saw me passing your way.

I smiled and asked if you would stay.
And you said okay.
Apparently, you'd been watching me for some time
and intended on making me yours anyway.

You mean to tell me this was meant to be,
and all this time we had no control.
You mean we were predestined to find each other,
and it was written from days of old.

We were made of the same material,
a patchwork pattern, put together,
nicely intertwined.
We were a perfect fit in my mind.

Penelope's Purple Passions

How can I create that moment again?
I want to feel that magic
of making love to you in the sand,
do you remember that day when?

I reached deep down into my bag of magic tricks,
just hoping and wishing I could relive that moment once more, rewind
My heart is still there
like a broken hand on the clock,
lost in time.

Escape

How do you escape a love?
That's a true dilemma.
A real twisted fate, it seems to me.

If it only ever existed in the spiritual realm,
how can you fully embrace it in its entirety?

Wouldn't the person need to be aware
of how much you loved them first?
Or could you just put your wish
out into the universe?

I put my love for you into the universe
before we even met.
I've always known you would find me.
I never doubted for a minute that we would come to be.

And although we're not together at this moment,
it doesn't mean we're not meant to be.

Nothing will ever keep our hearts from beating
to the rhythm of love;
our roots run too deep.

Lonely

I'm lonely this year.
I've really missed you.
    And it really hit me on my birthday.
An overwhelming sense of emptiness came over me.
I thought about the October we spent my
birthday together,
and a sense of sadness fell upon me.
The emptiness I feel from the lack of your presence
breaks me emotionally.
    Eventually, I will be able to get through the loss one day at a time.
I wonder if you even remember me.
Sometimes, I think that you might even think of me.
It happens mostly during the night.
This is the time when my mind is most at peace.
I feel like my spirit communicates with you vividly then.

I remember when we were happy way back when. I haven't spoken to you since then. I have to shake myself out of this lovestruck mentality. Sometimes, I say to myself, "Stop it, let them go, let it be. If they cared, even a little bit, they would contact you. Why do I still care?"

No Explanations

I don't want to stop loving you deeply,
and this makes no sense to me.
Why does a person have to exist unlinked
to the only thing that has ever made any sense?

I know it's hard to explain,
but this felt so real.
It was like love was the only earthly emotion
that I was supposed to feel.

How can a magnetic forcefield draw two people together
so tightly?
This feeling is one of total elation,
and it just felt right to me.

Release your grip then,
if we cannot be together.
Let me move on;
don't you think that would be better?

As usual, you intend to only serve your own
self-interests.
You don't care who you hurt,

just as long as everything lines itself up for you; that is
how you work.

You've set me up on the chessboard you've crafted.
You've played me like a rookie piece
and disposed of me,
just like all the other pieces you've drafted.

You move everyone around
and make them fall and disappear like smoke.
You cast your magic spell on your victims;
to you it's all a joke.

Or perhaps you like games and toying with your victims
before you go in for the kill,
leaving all the broken hearts on the side of the road
as you make your way through this town called
Brokenheartedville.

Now

Now that there's no one else around
I can finally exhale, sit down,
and listen to the raindrops beat against the windowpane.

Now that you've moved on and I will never see you
again, I can't believe it's actually happening.

After all this time of loving you secretly for years,
it's happened. I've come upon one of my worst fears.

In my mind, I can't find a reason or the time,
but I know in my heart that you've stopped trying.

I designed you in my mind, long before we even met.

It's been said, you can have anything you want if you can
visualize it.

Your dream will pursue you and overtake you
just like I've been wanting it to.
I don't want to quit.
I don't want to give up on it.

You're all I've ever wanted from the beginning.

But I sense you've moved on somehow,
like the gust of the wind.

And if I must let you go,
I sincerely want you to know,
your happiness is all I've ever wanted.
I don't need a special reason to love you,
I just do.

When I would sit and stare at the night sky,
the moon told me one day you would be in my life.

Although I thought our love would last forever and a day.

I know that you have your life to live, and I must let you
go your way.

The Pupa's Paradigm Shift

Looking back,
I could've loved you so hard—forever.

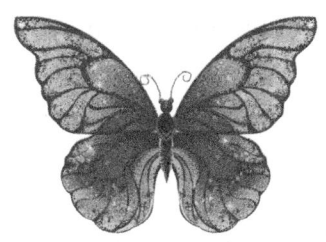

You Don't Know Me

You see, the thing about people is,
they think they know everything about me.

It's amazing to see and hear
all the things they think about me.

I don't know how they gather so much nonsense
in their heads about me.

Sometimes, I just sit and laugh
and entertain the thoughts they have about me.

To see myself in their eyes is quite amusing when I
consider what they think about me.

How can they believe that they know me with such
abstract information about me?

Don't you want me to fill in the holes, preferably
when it comes to me?

Perhaps I make what looks crazy seem sane,
or perhaps you like the gossip of what the people
are saying.

The Pupa's Paradigm Shift

Well, you made your choice as far as things go
concerning you and me.
Could it possibly be that I'm an amazing me?

Could it be the people were filled with jealousy and
envy of me?

In time, we shall see why they were filled with so much
resentment when it came to me.

We'll see when I'm on top
where everyone can see me,
which is where I was always predestined to be,
yes, ME.

Judged

You judged me the first time you got a chance. It's as though you were waiting for me to make a mistake. I was thinking more like me, you, and romance. It's funny how your mind can tell you all the things you'd like to hear. Most times, I think people make their judgments based on fear. You fear that the person you're fond of will hurt you, which compels you to hurt them first. You fear the other person's not perfect, leading your mind to drum up the worst. Why couldn't you think, *Maybe she's different, and I just don't quite understand her yet?* Why couldn't you think, *She's not perfect, but she's someone I can work with.*

Instead, you listened to what your friends told you, and you judged me without the slightest clue. And I'm sitting here wishing you knew. What I would do to have spent more time with you. Were you scared to be around me, just the two of us alone? Were you frightened that you would've liked me, and your vulnerability would have shown? But if I would've known you for just a minute or two, I'm quite sure we would've been magical. We have so many things in common that you never got to discover, so many moments that could have been uncovered. And now, my mind says no wonder. It turned out to be a big blunder. But oh, how I wish I could've known you for a minute or two.

A Fool

I saw you walking the other day; you looked so confident and cool. You even had an extra dip in your step, and I know what that meant too. I know you're seeing someone. I'm not sure when you started dating them, or when your love affair had begun. All I can tell you is that the way you're looking at me, they are definitely not the one. Don't look at me with that seductive smile you love to give; I thought that we were done. You're trying to break down all my defenses.

Don't think that I don't know what you're trying to do. You played me like an idiot when I was gullible. Because of my experience with you, I've grown up now and learned the game. I know now how to move to the left and the right to duck your aim. You can look and find yourself a lonely heart to sink your vicious, slick claws into. I've moved on now; my priorities are in order. I'm no longer into you.

The Joke's on Me

Every time I think about you
and your friends laughing it up about how you hurt me,
a red-hot fire runs through my veins.

You mean to tell me this is the same person
I thought I was in love with and once entertained?

How could I not have seen all of this?
Does love really make you this sick?

If so, I don't want to love anymore.
I'm done with it.

The joke's on me.
I was the butt of all your jokes, a real court jester
without the costume, you see.

Feelings of rage, anger, hurt, and self-pity,
all rolled up into this monstrous giant ball.
Every time I see you, it's as though I'm reliving it all.

Day after day, I'm tormented thinking about all the jokes
you and your friends made at my expense,
and I didn't have a clue.

Yes, that's me, the court jester, the biggest clown of them all.
And in the end, I did fall.

Unfortunately, I fell for you.

Blind

It felt like a sharp dagger,
the blow that separated the left side of my heart
from the right.

There was no fair warning,
not a sign of danger in sight.

That was the night of all nights.

I realized from the way you now addressed me
that I was no longer the moon in your life,
your provider of light.

Someone else had caught your attention,
and now our fairy-tale love
would no longer be mentioned
in all of the love stories like *Romeo and Juliet*.

How did I not see this?

What could I've done any differently
to help you not forget?
Perhaps there was nothing to be done.
What if you were not destined for me?

Perhaps all the signs were there,
and I was just way too busy
enjoying the ride and adventure
that I didn't see the obvious signs
as they passed by.

Maybe I should have never loved you
spontaneously.

Perhaps love is not blind, and
now I've learned why.

Love

Love just is.

I say, let love be what it is destined to be.

We spend so much time trying to define love.

What is this thing called love?

Is there an expiration date on it
or some sort of timeline?

Why must we put labels, restrictions,
and perform fancy calculations
to add up the cost before we dive in?

Just let go, give it all you've got,
and enjoy the ride.
Express what you're feeling,
be free to let the other person inside.

Open yourself up to endless possibilities
You never know,
if you love hard and strong enough,
it could turn out to be something beautiful.

Penelope's Purple Passions

At least, that's what I thought when I met you.
In the end, though, it was all for naught.
It fell through.

But at least I dove in and gave it all I had.
 You only live once in this life,
even if your love is not reciprocated
and the ending is bad.

Truth

The truth is,
it doesn't matter how many times
my heart gets broken,
as long as my truth has been spoken.

If I've learned and grown as a person
from all of my life's encounters,
I've obtained it all.

And that truth, my friend,
is simply divine.
I've lived my life to the fullest
and answered love's call.

The Zone

Sometimes, I feel like I'm out here
in this thing we call existence all alone.

I often withdraw into my own
wonderfully constructed sanctuary
called the quiet zone.

I watch the people pass by,
coming from places I don't know.

Who can really know where all these people go?

Oftentimes, I just look at them with a blank stare.

They think I'm looking at them,
but I really don't care.

I'm off in my own world,
thinking of you sometimes.

I'm in this place called the zone.

That's where you invade my mind.

Am I the crazy one?

How can being in this state of reverie be fun?
I'm just sitting here on this bench at noon
taking life in, soaking up the warm rays
from the reddish-orange sun.

It's during these times of daydreaming,
I find my solace, my lasting peace, my true home.

This is where I've retreated now,
since that day you signed off and left me all alone.

The zone.

Thinking

I was thinking,
I need someone bold in my life.
But am I bold?

So many years of being everything to everyone else,
how can I ask for such daring actions from others that I
myself am not willing to take?
Maybe this is all a big mistake.

I mean, I've wanted to say so many things to you,
and I've let the moments slip by like passing trains.
And as I look back on my life,
that's been one of my many shames.

All to realize, maybe,
I'm asking you to set something free in me
that I simply cannot do.
Maybe I expected way too much from you.
But no one person
can be expected to set you free.

No, I don't think I have it in me.
Yes, it's true.

You are free, and I'm a coward.
Just look at me.

I cannot ask you to love me deeply
if I'm holding back.

It's true I don't have it in me.
You were right about me.

The Airport

They told me to write about
what I thought love was.
But when I began to reflect,
all I could see was you.

The only picture that came to my mind
was your face.

I want to stop time.
I want to go back to that day.
I looked up in the Louis Armstrong international airport,
and you were there, staring, just smiling at me.

I don't know how to explain it,
but my heart became happy inside.
Your smile hides words
that I'd never heard uttered before.

How did you do that with just a smile?
It was like enchantment or something,
the way it left me helpless, like a child.

After all, it's all your fault,
this mess you made.

The Pupa's Paradigm Shift

Look at what you put me through.
You're the one who beguiled me,
making me fall helplessly in love with you.

Write Back When You Get My Letter

By the time you write back to me,
it will be too late.
I was your should've been,
you didn't appreciate.

I guess loss can be a good thing.
Loss helps you identify what was good
and helps you make wiser choices over time.

Down the line, I met someone
who reminded me of a choice like you.

And I ran.
I remembered all the pain you caused,
the way you pillaged through my life
like a tumultuous storm.

You brought in all of your chaotic self,
like a whirlwind.
With the same vigor,
you whisked right out of my life.

The Pupa's Paradigm Shift

I was left to pick up all the broken pieces.
I didn't know how to start rebuilding.

How do you put something as fragile
as a heart back together?
How can you recover
from the tropical storm-like weather?

You just begin picking up all the loose branches,
like the day after a storm, one branch at a time.
Piece by piece you begin to rebuild,
laying one brick down at a time.

Next time,
I'll make sure to have a sturdier foundation,
a back-up, a lifeline.
That way, I'll be prepared
for any tropical storm
and be able to take cover.

It took me so long after loving you
to rearrange all my heart's closed window shutters.

I built myself up brick by brick.
And it took me quite some time;
it was far from quick.

Penelope's Purple Passions

I learned my lesson,
and there's one thing I know to be true.
The next time I see a storm like you coming,
I'll know what to do.

Lay With It

If I take away
the fact that I ever knew you,
then I take away that metaphysical connection we made,
   unforgettable moments filled with bliss.

No, that's too precious.
This is just between us two

I think I will just lay with it,
   if only for a few.

No Delete Button

You think you're over me,
but you're not.
I wasn't what your friends wanted,
but I was what you got.

I'm definitely a fact you'll never be able to erase.
You will always be haunted by my face.
I don't care how many romance books you write.
I'll always be the love of your life.

Now when you close your eyes
and see visions of me in your dreams,
I want you to know that I represent what true
love means.

Your Loss

I chose to close myself off to the world
after you left and never spoke to me again.
It's because you hurt me
and left me with a desolate feeling.

The loss of you took me to deep dark places.
My spirit was torn apart, but I knew I had to face this.
Something about seeing you with that other woman,
and you even looked as if you were glowing.

I felt as though you had never really cared about me,
and it was definitely showing.
You moved on in what, a few weeks maybe,
without me even knowing.

I wasn't able to quite understand how.
It took me a while to digest it all,
but I got my groove back now
after I processed it all.

You see me, high-stepping now, baby,
no love lost over here.
I stepped out of the fear
and began a new year.

Penelope's Purple Passions

I overcame this devastation
and paid a hefty cost.
I'm out here making major moves now, baby,
and it is, and will always be, your loss.

Morning Comes

I feel good this morning. A couple of eggs and some freshly brewed coffee. Coffee has a way of making everything better. I feel like I might be able to finally let it all go. I've finally gotten past the hurt—no more teary eyes, no more thoughts of wondering why. I used a warm towel with a bit of hot steam to remove the crust from the cracks of my eyelids after I arose this morning. Oh, how I dread getting up early in the morning. I have to deal with all the idiots on the road. I'm now yelling all the f...s as these crazy idiots race on the road like drunk drivers. And I'm saying, "Lord, please don't let me have a crazy day today." Took my shower, check. Brushed my teeth, check. Packed my lunch bag, check. Workout bag ready, check. Almost forgot my earrings, that's a no-no, check. And I'm off to the rat race with all of the rest of the working-class zombies.

Ghosts

I thank every love in my life who ghosted me.
It turned out to be quite a blessing.
The hurt I endured taught me valuable lessons.

My light and love
should not be given out so openly and freely.
But without the pain
from all of my loves of yesterday,
the world would not know the new me.

I took all of those times,
I wondered why they hurt me,
and turned them into opportunities.

I took all of those moments, I wondered why they did
what they did, and used them to inspire my comebacks.

I took all of those times
they left me for dead
to create beautiful poetry in my head.

I stand here strong; I survived the fight.
I'm the beautiful black-and-yellow monarch butterfly
ready to take her first flight.

The Adult's Climax

Sorry

It was the hurt that kept me alive. It made me strong enough to get past the anger and survive. The pain you left me in when you took off was unbearable. It was as though you couldn't care less about how I would feel. The absence of your sweet aroma, carnation skin, and raven black hair. One minute, you were here in my arms and the next there, somewhere else. Did you take a minute to even think before you walked away? Probably not, not even a maybe. I know you never anticipated you would ever see this day, when I would rise up, a beautiful phoenix reborn, and stretch my wings across the earth like the bright sun's rays.

But life is just that way. When you beat someone down, expect that someday they will recover and make a grand comeback. The next time you saw me you looked shocked. You didn't know how to react. For I had become what I always was. You just didn't stick around to find out. You left, just because. I'll perhaps never know why and always doubt. Now when you see me, you can't really look me in the eyes; it's as though you're ashamed. After all, you were the one who caused me so much pain. I'm not sure what you gained, maybe some unknown fame.

To me, it was like the whole time you were playing a game. There were no apologies left to give, no heartfelt goodbyes. I just had the tears you caused, which filled my bloodshot eyes. And after all these years, I thought you would've mustered up the courage to say you were sorry for all the pain you caused. But no, not you, the most sadistic person there ever was.

Let Go

I read a quote today, and it simply said life gets so much simpler once you give up on people who don't respect your efforts toward them. It reminded me of how I used to be, always wanting to see the best in everyone and what I thought they could be. The only one who ended up hurt was me. When I let everyone go and began to fall in love with what loved me, I experienced what it was like to really be free. The flowers started to bloom in spring.

My life took off with a sense of newness and fulfilled meaning. You mean to tell me, all this time, that was all I had to do—let go of you and whomever didn't care about me too? Wow, this was a real enlightening moment if I must say so myself. I'm loving myself now more than I'm loving anyone else.

Rainbows

I saw a double rainbow in the sky one day. People say double rainbows are a rare thing to see. It kind of reminds me of me. I felt like it was reassuring me everything was going to be okay for me someday. Anyway, I didn't stay. I was sitting in traffic and had to continue on my way. I kept driving down the road taking in all of nature's glory, not knowing at that time what would become of my story. After the rain, we get rainbows, right? After the darkness, the earth brings forth light, right? But tonight, I was feeling like it was a self-reflection kind of night. What would be my life's plight? What was in store for me on this new day.

After all, the rainbows had promised me my new beginning. I didn't imagine I would be winning the way I was winning. Who would have predicted this after all the turmoil in my life? The heartbreaks, the disappointments, they all led me to this place. The place where the rainbows end, that's where I was to start my new beginning. What a magnificent road. All the beautiful experiences that are already set up for me to behold. I've had amazing encounters bursting with excitement, much like that of the bright colors that burst from the rainbow—a life so full of adventure and the fulfillment of my childhood fantasies. The rainbows represented a glimpse of hope and a wonderful life well lived as my perfect version of me.

Destiny

If you would've asked me even one year ago if I could've seen myself in this space. I would've said no. I never knew where to go, what I was destined for, or what road I was supposed to take. I was always making the same mistakes. Like a merry-go-round. I was always finding myself in the same sorts of situations that left me looking like a clown.

Why do I set myself up like this time and time again? Why do I keep placing myself in games I know I can't win? That's who I was, and I'm sure some of you can identify with being there. Going through the motions of this thing called life without a care. But then one day, you wake up. And it's as though there's this burning in your soul. You begin to think to yourself, *I want more. What am I here for?* Then you get these hints from the universe: go this way and look out for that. Facts start to pop up, and things start to make sense and fall into place. And then, as time goes on, you notice that you've changed.

Your life has been rearranged, and you are this new being. People are commenting on what they're seeing.

The "you" that was always there has now become aware.
The gifts within you are now ripe and ready to be shared.

Madness, Maybe

My real friends don't think I'm crazy;
that's what I love about them.

I daydream sometimes, when I'm alone,
and make decisions on a whim.

You have to understand
the complexity of how my mind works
to be able to keep up with me.

You have to be comfortable
with being uncomfortable, totally free.

I bring mystery, excitement,
and I make you ask yourself hard questions.

Just when you think you have me figured out, I will
cause you to start second-guessing

It's all in the process of self-discovery
I've started to challenge myself, which has become
a blessing

Penelope's Purple Passions

This is a part of my own evolution.
I'm not looking to make impressions.

I'm just letting my thoughts and creativity flow
like the water in a gentle, cool stream.

I feel hopeful about all the amazing possibilities
this life can bring
I feel like a sunflower flaunting its beauty in spring.

Unfamiliar Face

Unbelievable, that's what I thought to myself.
You passed right by me today at the coffee stand
and acted as if I never existed.
   I wondered why.

I'm pretty sure you knew it was me,
   but you walked right past, swiftly.

I wonder what makes a person so empty and cold.
Is this what happens as people grow old?

Perhaps it's all the mean and cruel things
they've done over the years
that they now have to live with.
Perhaps it's that the person they once loved
has moved on,
and now they are starting to feel it.

Well, I had to move on.
Life was pulling me forward, out of my past,
and into my present reality.
I had to give myself the chance to love someone
who truly loved me.

Penelope's Purple Passions

A person who brought out the gifts in me
and inspired me in ways I have never known.

Yes, I must say,
looking at myself now,
in comparison to three years ago,
I've certainly grown.

I'm not the delicate flower I used to be.
Now, I'm a more confident flower
emitting a sweet-smelling fragrance,
which can be picked up across eternity.

I'm finally free.

I feel light on my feet,
like I'm floating.
I'm glowing and it's showing.

I'm the beacon of light
that led my new lover safely
to meet me at the lighthouse.
No more wandering about.

I'm here now,
and I'm enjoying this newfound love.
If it's but for a moment it doesn't matter because
it is what I've always dreamed of.

So, I will conclude this moment and put my special seal on it.

I think I will sign this moment as simply magnificent.

Seven Years

Well, now that I have those long, grueling seven years under my belt,
now more than ever, I can distinguish through my practice of daily meditation what's real and what was never felt.

Friends have come and gone, and some bonds were torn.
And I, the butterfly,
was left with a feeling of scorn.

Not being able to realize the unforeseen blessing
of all the trials and what I felt was done to me
was really the essence of what had set me free.
I emerged with a new sense of life,
an amazing new identity.

I learned how to decipher the truth between the lies.
I learned to look a person right in the eyes;
this way they would not be able to hide or disguise their disloyalty to me
and what a true friendship is supposed to be.

I learned to only give the best of my love
to where it was given to me.

The Adult's Climax

A close friend of mine told me,
"You should only bleed for those who bleed for you."
It was quite an interesting concept.
And I embraced it and lived by it too.

I learned how to move on and wish all beings the
best in life.
I learned there was so much life to be lived
versus walking around with strife.

I learned to focus on me
and how to make my twenty-four hours count.

I learned that touching people's lives
and serving as a positive inspiration
is what life's all about.

Life's about living, enjoying laughter with friends,
and even anger sometimes.
It's about adventure and exhausting all the gifts
we've been given inside.

It's not about pride,
but about living a full life with each breath we take.
Life's about all the beauty we encounter
and the magnificent connections we make.

Wednesday

It's Wednesday, and although it's the middle of the week, I'm feeling so special. I'm in the middle of making big changes in my life. I'm breaking through some of my life's biggest achievements. I'm not alarmed by the chaos in the world or it's movements. I exist in my own world inside of my mind. I'm inviting in a new promise of a better version of me. I like this new woman; she's so confident and present, and she's in tune with everything around her. But at the same time, she's shielded from all of the madness in the world that would like to blind her. As the moments turn into hours and the days turn into years, the old me has somehow disappeared and someone else has emerged.

When I look in the mirror, I can't see any traces of the person I once was. Is it because I'm growing into this newfound creature? People are saying I have this glow about me. Really, tell me what it is you see? They say I'm different and they can't really put words on what they're seeing. But what they do know is that they see traces of this magnificent new human being. And so it is, the butterfly has now made an appearance. What was set in stone from the beginning of time is emerging without interference. What is meant to be can never be stopped.

The Adult's Climax

You cannot drop your destiny, for it is forever calling and summoning you to come forth to the front. First, I must be the butterfly that I was predestined and called to be from birth.

New Leaf

I turned over a new leaf in my old age,
and all of a sudden, I wanted to do something different.

Perhaps I shouldn't say different.
Somehow, what had always been
didn't seem to fit the puzzle within.

Somehow, I wanted more adventure in my life,
to be free to explore.

The possibilities are numerous and wide open for me.
I can see, with every move I make,
something great awaits.

So why not now, why not today?
Isn't today and this hour as good as any?

I love this new hold I have on life,
and how it has me feeling.

I feel like drinking lots of coffee
at all hours of the night and day.

The Adult's Climax

I feel like traveling the world
and staying wherever I want to stay.

I feel like all this time I was waiting on the world,
the whole universe was waiting on me,
to take flight, spread my wings, and let the butterfly

within me, roam freely.

Impression

My life was filled with so many things I should've done
Then one day, I decided to do all the things I could do
and even what others said couldn't be done.

It's been a fun run.

I will never again let myself listen to anyone.
Especially if what they have to say
tries to deter me and make me change my mind.

I'm here to leave a lasting impact on this world,
and it's my time to shine.

I will take all the risks this time.
If I fail,
    it'll just drive me to press on even harder next time.

I now flow with what pleases me,
    whatever comes to mind.

I will never again be that person
questioning what could've been.
I'll be the butterfly who changes the world around her
and makes things happen.

The Adult's Climax

I guess I will name myself butterfly proactive.
Yes, perhaps I will, I think it sounds attractive.

If nothing else, nobody will ever forget my name.
I will leave a lasting impression in this life;
no one in this universe was created the same.

Thankful

I'm thankful for all my experiences with love and life. Without these experiences what would I draw from? What would I have to write? I've learned so much about life, love, and relationships along this journey. Some things I had to see and experience for myself; nobody could have warned me. There is so much growth and knowledge obtained through one's own personal experiences along the way. I've learned to give love and life my best efforts every day. But in giving, I've also learned to make wiser choices in my life than I used to make. I've learned to stay away from people and situations that could cause me to break. But I've also learned love can be beautiful if experienced with the right person. I've learned you may have to encounter many relationships before you encounter this love and not to settle for the first one.

Butterfly Wings

The butterfly withdrew from the life she knew,
not knowing how she would pick up the pieces of her
heart again.

She was broken. She hadn't spoken.
Not in years.

She had to go to a place nobody knows,
the place all broken butterflies go.

They go there to have their wings repaired,
or perhaps replaced, whatever it takes.

There are wings there
of all different colors and shapes.

It's there that she can start anew
and transform into a new beautiful creature.

Nobody recognized her because she had developed
completely new features.
Everyone wondered where she went.
She was a broken butterfly, hurt and innocent.

She had to recover and embrace this new being she
had become.
She had to spend time loving herself away
from everyone.

You won't recognize the butterfly now,
    such magnificent wings with which she is adorned.

Just when you thought she was done,
she rose up and won.

And there she was, bright and beautiful,
    smiling and flapping her new butterfly wings.

About Penelope Chaisson

Penelope Chaisson is a Louisiana native who has been writing poetry for over 30 years. Despite the demanding career as a nurse anesthetist and nationals strong woman athlete, her passion for poetry has never waned. Penelope's Purple Passions is her debut collection of poems.

For more information about Penelope's writings and projects visit penelopespassages.com

---

To learn more about Evoke180 Publishing visit our website
www.evoke180.com

Made in United States
Orlando, FL
27 February 2024